EXPLORE THE PLANETS

BY EMMA HUDDLESTON

CONTENT CONSULTANT
LARRY ESPOSITO, PhD
PROFESSOR, ASTROPHYSICAL AND PLANETARY SCIENCES
UNIVERSITY OF COLORADO BOULDER

Kids Core

An Imprint of Abdo Publishing
abdobooks.com

abdobooks.com

Published by Abdo Publishing, a division of ABDO, PO Box 398166, Minneapolis, Minnesota 55439. Copyright © 2022 by Abdo Consulting Group, Inc. International copyrights reserved in all countries. No part of this book may be reproduced in any form without written permission from the publisher. Kids Core™ is a trademark and logo of Abdo Publishing.

Printed in the United States of America, North Mankato, Minnesota
052021
092021

THIS BOOK CONTAINS
RECYCLED MATERIALS

Cover Photo: ESA/NASA
Interior Photos: JPL/NASA, 4–5, 6, 8, 12, 18; JPL/Space Science Institute/NASA, 9; Caltech/Palomar Observatory/NASA, 10; JHU/APL/NASA, 11; JPL-CalTech/NASA, 14–15; JPL-Caltech/MSSS/NASA, 16; iStockphoto, 17; Science Source, 20; Oliver Kufner/iStockphoto, 22–23; SCIEPRO/Science Source, 25; Shutterstock Images, 26, 28–29

Editor: Marie Pearson
Series Designer: Katharine Hale

Library of Congress Control Number: 2020948355

Publisher's Cataloging-in-Publication Data

Names: Huddleston, Emma, author.
Title: Explore the planets / by Emma Huddleston
Description: Minneapolis, Minnesota : Abdo Publishing, 2022 | Series: Explore space! | Includes online resources and index.
Identifiers: ISBN 9781532195396 (lib. bdg.) | ISBN 9781644945438 (pbk.) | ISBN 9781098215705 (ebook)
Subjects: LCSH: Outer space--Exploration--Juvenile literature. | Planets--Juvenile literature. | Solar system--Juvenile literature. | Astronomy--Juvenile literature.
Classification: DDC 523.4--dc23

CONTENTS

The solar system is often shown with the planets much closer to the Sun than they really are.

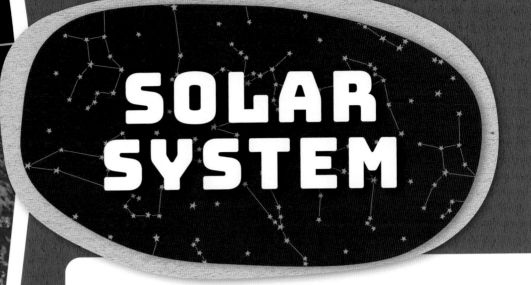

CHAPTER 1

SOLAR SYSTEM

The Sun is a star. It is the center of our solar system. It sends energy in the form of light to eight planets around it. One of those planets is Earth. The Sun allows people and other living things to thrive.

Each planet is unique.

The other seven planets are each a bit different. Some are rocky like Earth. Others are made of gas. Some are hot. Others are cold. Together, they make up the solar system. A solar system includes a star and the bodies that circle around it.

What Are Planets?

Planets are in space. A planet is defined by three main things. First, it **orbits** a star. Second, it is large enough that gravity makes it round. Gravity is a force that pulls smaller objects to the center of a very large object in space. Third, the planet's gravity must influence all other objects in its orbital path.

Part of a Galaxy

The solar system is part of a galaxy. A galaxy is made up of many stars and their systems. It can have different shapes, such as a **spiral**. Earth's solar system is in the Milky Way galaxy.

Venus, *pictured*, is only a tiny bit smaller than Earth.

Our solar system has eight planets. Mercury is nearest the Sun. But it is not the hottest. The next planet, Venus, is hottest. Its surface temperatures reach 900 degrees Fahrenheit (465°C). Earth is third in line. It is special because it is the only known planet with life. Mars is next. It is a red, dusty planet.

Fifth from the Sun is Jupiter. Jupiter is the largest planet. Its **mass** is twice as big as all the others together. Saturn and its beautiful rings are sixth. Next is Uranus.

People can view Saturn's rings from Earth using a personal telescope.

It gets little heat. Neptune is the eighth and farthest planet from the Sun. It is 2.8 billion miles (4.5 billion km) away. Methane gas in the air makes Uranus and Neptune look blue.

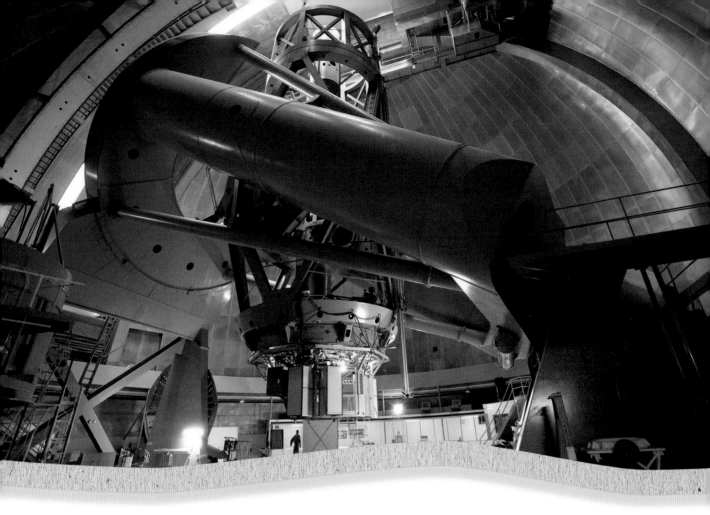

Some large scientific telescopes are kept inside observatories. The roof can open so the telescope can view the sky.

Exploring Space

Scientists study space with telescopes. Telescopes are tools that use mirrors and glass to gather light. They **magnify** the planets. Scientists also study space with probes. Probes are machines sent into space on a specific path. Some fly around planets. They send close images of the planet to people on Earth.

Messenger was a space probe sent to photograph Mercury.

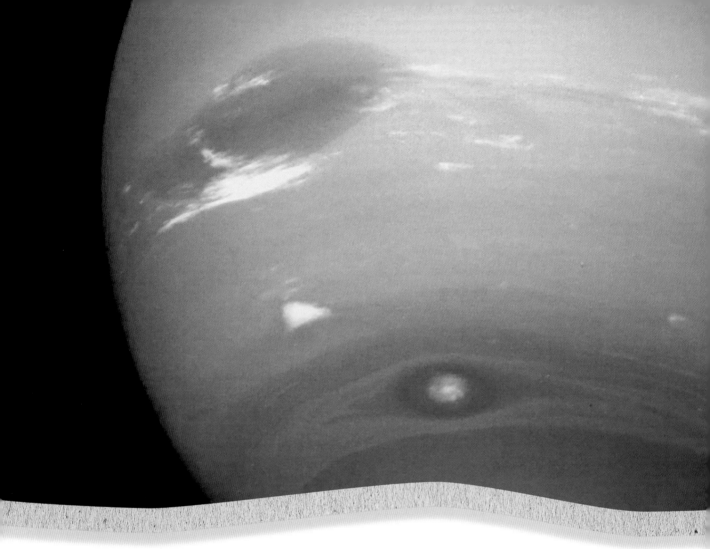

Streaks and swirls on a gas planet, such as
Neptune, show air currents and storms.

Exploring the planets can be difficult because
they are far from Earth. Scientists learn about
their size, their temperature, and what they are
made of. This helps scientists understand planet
Earth even better.

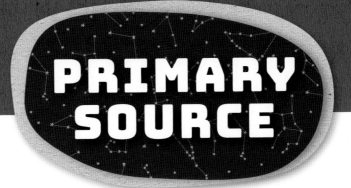

Nicky Fox of NASA explains challenges to exploring space. The Sun releases ionizing radiation, which is energy that is dangerous to anyone outside Earth's **atmosphere**. Fox said:

> We not only have to ensure our astronauts are protected from the harmful effects of radiation. We have to protect our equipment too.

Source: "Effects of the Solar Wind." *NASA Science*, 24 Nov. 2019, science.nasa.gov. Accessed 30 Apr. 2020.

What's the Big Idea?

Read this quote carefully. What is its main idea? Explain how the main idea is supported by details.

Planets form out of material
that is orbiting a star.

CHAPTER 2

ROCK AND GAS

Planets form out of gas and dust. Eventually, gravity pulls chunks of rock and gas together. If the object is large enough, it forms the matter into a **sphere**. Planets can be made of many types of materials.

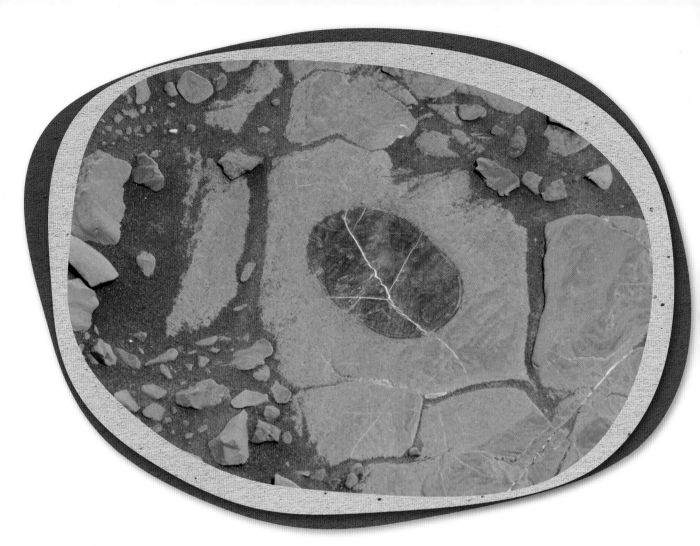

Scientists send special land vehicles called rovers to Mars. The rovers can take close-up pictures of Mars's surface.

Rocky Planets

The smallest planets, and those closest to the Sun, are rocky. They are made of different kinds of metals and rocks. A rocky planet's **crust**

Earth's crust supports life.

is hard. In Earth's solar system, the rocky planets are Mercury, Venus, Earth, and Mars. Mercury is the smallest planet in the solar system. It is about three times smaller than Earth.

People only have to step outside to see Earth's rocky crust. It forms mountains, plains, and the ocean floor.

Earth's atmosphere is visible from space. It appears as a blue haze above the planet.

Planets can have thick or thin **atmospheres**. An atmosphere is the layer of gas around a planet. Venus has a thick atmosphere. It traps lots of heat. It makes the planet very hot. Mars has a thin atmosphere. Its surface is colder and dusty. Earth's atmosphere is made of gases that living things can breathe. It keeps the planet the right temperature for life. It is not too thick or too thin.

Gas Planets

The four outer planets are known as gas giants. They are Jupiter, Saturn, Uranus, and Neptune. Gas giants may have small, rocky cores deep inside. But they are mostly made of swirling gases, liquids, and dust. They don't have a hard crust like rocky planets have. The gas giants are the largest planets.

Pluto

Pluto was called the ninth planet from 1930 to 2006. In 2006, scientists determined it was a dwarf planet. A dwarf planet is smaller than a planet. It orbits the Sun and is not a moon. Its gravity is strong enough to make it a round shape. But its gravity is too weak to clear the area in its orbital path.

This image compares the size difference between Earth and Jupiter.

Jupiter is the largest planet. If it were a basketball, Earth would be a golf ball. Saturn is a gas giant famous for its rings. Its rings are made of chunks of rock and ice. However, Saturn isn't the only planet with rings. All gas giants have them. Rocky planets do not.

Uranus and Neptune are icy gas giants. They are blue and windy. They have colder temperatures because they are so far from the Sun's heat. Uranus is colder than Neptune in some places.

Explore Online

Visit the website below. Does it give any new information about planets that wasn't in Chapter Two?

All About the Planets

abdocorelibrary.com/explore-the -planets

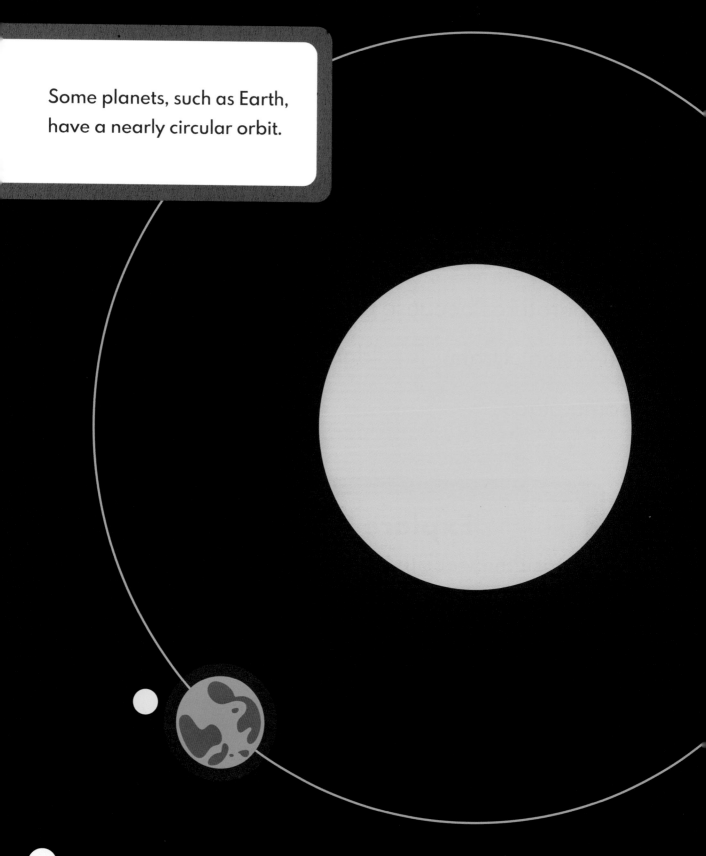

Some planets, such as Earth, have a nearly circular orbit.

CHAPTER 3

SPINNING IN ORBIT

Planets orbit the Sun. They follow curved paths as they orbit. The Sun's gravity keeps them from drifting off into space. The time it takes a planet to make one full orbit around the Sun is one year on that planet.

Planets located close to the Sun have shorter years. Neptune is the farthest planet, so it takes the longest to travel around the Sun. One trip is as long as 165 Earth years.

Spinning

While orbiting the Sun, a planet also spins on its axis. An axis is an imaginary line that runs through the center of a planet. Jupiter spins

Moons

Moons are objects that orbit some planets. They are smaller than the planet they orbit. Earth has one moon. Saturn has more than 80. Scientists are still discovering all of Saturn's moons. Since gas giants have larger bodies, their gravity is stronger. They have more moons than the smaller rocky planets.

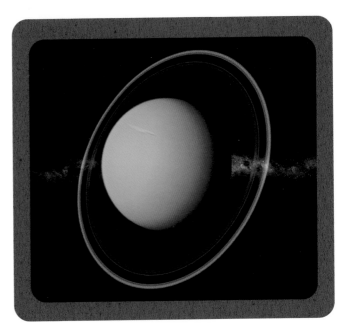

Faint rings around Uranus show the angle at which the planet spins.

nearly perfectly straight up and down. Uranus is sometimes called the sideways planet because it spins on its side.

Earth's axis is slightly **tilted**. The tilt causes seasons. In northern summer, the North Pole is angled toward the Sun. Earth's northern half gets more direct sunlight than the south. This makes the north warm. Other times the South Pole is angled toward the Sun. Then Earth's southern half is warmer.

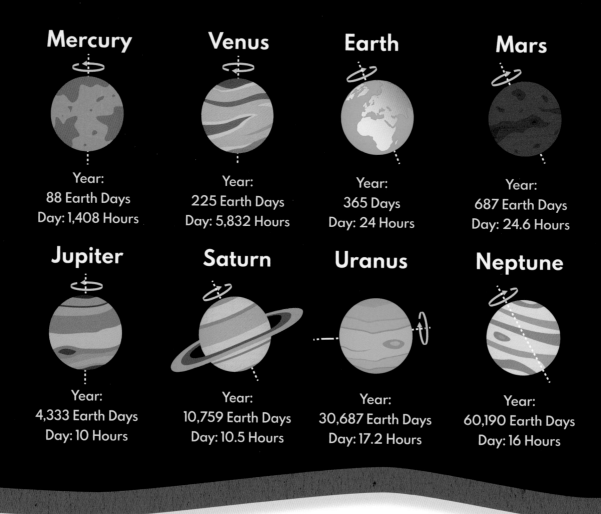

Mercury	Venus	Earth	Mars
Year: 88 Earth Days Day: 1,408 Hours	**Year:** 225 Earth Days Day: 5,832 Hours	**Year:** 365 Days Day: 24 Hours	**Year:** 687 Earth Days Day: 24.6 Hours
Jupiter	**Saturn**	**Uranus**	**Neptune**
Year: 4,333 Earth Days Day: 10 Hours	**Year:** 10,759 Earth Days Day: 10.5 Hours	**Year:** 30,687 Earth Days Day: 17.2 Hours	**Year:** 60,190 Earth Days Day: 16 Hours

This image shows the length of day and year for each planet in the solar system. Some are much longer than Earth's days and years. Others are much shorter.

The amount of time it takes for a planet to complete one spin on its axis determines the length of a day. On Earth, this takes 24 hours.

Saturn spins faster. Its days last only 10.5 hours. Venus spins slowly. A day on Venus takes 5,832 hours.

The planets are some of the largest bodies in the solar system besides the Sun. Each one is unique. Some are rocky and small. Others are gas giants. Exploring the planets in space leads to many new discoveries!

Further Evidence

Visit the website below. Does it give any new information about orbits that wasn't in Chapter Three?

Earth's Orbit

abdocorelibrary.com/explore-the -planets

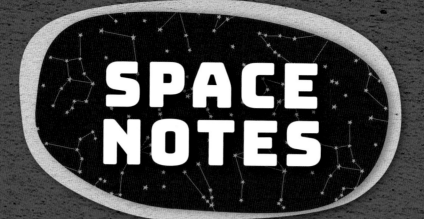

SPACE NOTES

Mercury

Venus   Earth   Mars

Sun

Rocky Planets

Jupiter

Uranus

Neptune

Saturn

Gas Planets

Glossary

atmosphere
a protective layer of gas around an object in space

crust
a hard, rocky surface layer of a planet

magnify
to zoom in on something or make it appear larger

mass
a measure of how much matter is in an object

orbits
follows an oval-shaped path around a larger object

sphere
an object with a round, ball-like shape

spiral
a shape with parts twisting out from the center

tilted
leaned to one side

Online Resources

To learn more about the planets, visit our free resource websites below.

Visit **abdocorelibrary.com** or scan this QR code for free Common Core resources for teachers and students, including vetted activities, multimedia, and booklinks, for deeper subject comprehension.

Visit **abdobooklinks.com** or scan this QR code for free additional online weblinks for further learning. These links are routinely monitored and updated to provide the most current information available.

Learn More

Baines, Rebecca. *Planets*. National Geographic Kids, 2016.

Huddleston, Emma. *Explore the Sun*. Abdo Publishing, 2022.

Woodward, John. *Super Earth Encyclopedia*. DK, 2017.

Index

About the Author

Emma Huddleston lives in Minnesota with her husband.
She enjoys writing books for young readers and staying
active. She thinks learning about space is fascinating!